Guide

KANSAS

By Carole Marsh

The GALLOPADE GANG

Carole Marsh
Bob Longmeyer
Chad Beard
Cecil Anderson
Steven Saint-Laurent
Jill Sanders
Kathy Zimmer
Terry Briggs
Pat Newman
Billie Walburn
Jackie Clayton
Pam Dufresne
Cranston Davenport
Lisa Stanley
Antoinette Miller
Victoria DeJoy
Al Fortunatti
Shery Kearney

Published by GALLOPADE INTERNATIONAL

www.kansasexperience.com
800-536-2GET • www.gallopade.com

Gallopade is proud to be a member of these educational organizations and associations:

Other Kansas Experience Products

- The Kansas Experience!
- The BIG Kansas Reproducible Activity Book
- The Kansas Coloring Book
- My First Book About Kansas!
- Kansas "Jography": A Fun Run Through Our State
- Kansas Jeopardy!: Answers and Questions About Our State
- The Kansas Experience! Sticker Pack
- The Kansas Experience! Poster/Map
- Discover Kansas CD-ROM
- Kansas "Geo" Bingo Game
- Kansas "Histo" Bingo Game

A Word From the Author... (okay, a few words)...

Hi!

Here's your own handy pocket guide about the great state of Kansas! It really will fit in a pocket—I tested it. And it really will be useful when you want to know a fact you forgot, to bone up for a test, or when your teacher says, "I wonder . . ." and you have the answer—instantly! Wow, I'm impressed!

Get smart, have fun!

Carole Marsh

Kansas Basics explores your state's symbols and their special meanings!

Kansas Geography digs up the what's where in your state!

Kansas History is like traveling through time to some of your state's great moments!

Kansas People introduces you to famous personalities and your next-door neighbors!

Kansas Places shows you where you might enjoy your next family vacation!

Kansas Nature - no preservatives here, just what Mother Nature gave to Kansas!

All the real fun stuff that we just HAD to save for its own section!

Who Named You?

Kansas' official state name is...

Kansas

State Name

OFFICIAL: appointed, authorized, or approved by a government or organization

Statehood:

January 29,1861

Kansas was the 34th state to join the Union.

Kansas will be on a state-commemorative quarter starting in the year 2005. Look for it in cash registers everywhere!

What's In A Name?

Kansas got its name from the Sioux word for people of the "south wind." The Sioux Indians once roamed the Great Plains.

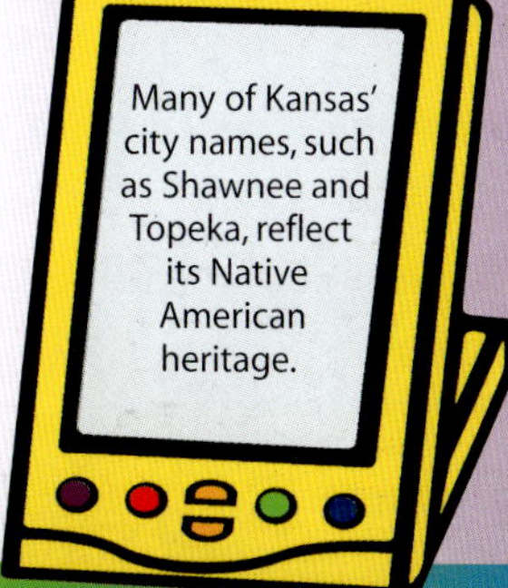

WHO Are You Calling Names?

Kansas is not the only name by which our state is recognized. Like many other states, Kansas has some nicknames, official or unofficial!

State Capital: TOPEKA

Established: 1854

Capital of Kansas since: 1861

The New England Aid Society organized groups of people to move west into Kansas. The settlers came to Topeka in 1854. The area was incorporated as a city in 1857.

Topeka was chosen to be a railroad center in the early days of its settlement. It was also considered to be a "free-soil" center for those who opposed slavery in the region.

The state capitol building was built of native limestone in 1866.

Word Definition

CAPITAL: a town or city that is the official seat of government

CAPITOL: the building in which the government officials meet

Who's in Charge Here?

Kansas' GOVERNMENT has three branches:

EXECUTIVE	LEGISLATIVE	JUDICIAL
A governor, lieutenant governor, secretary of state, attorney general, state treasurer, and commissioner of insurance	Two Houses: The Senate (40 members) House of Representatives (125 members)	Supreme Court, chief justice and six other justices Court of appeals, ten members District courts, thirty-one courts

The number of legislators is determined by population, which is counted every ten years; the numbers above are certain to change as Kansas grows and prospers!

When you are 18 and register according to Kansas laws, you can vote! So please do! Your vote counts!

State Flag

KANSAS

Kansas' current state flag was adopted in 1927. It features a sunflower atop the state seal on a blue background. Under the sunflower there is a blue and gold bar symbolizing that Kansas was part of the Louisiana Purchase. In 1961 the word Kansas was added to the flag at the bottom.

As you travel throughout Kansas, count the times you see the Kansas flag! Look for it on government vehicles, too!

State Seal

The state seal of Kansas features a landscape with the sun rising to represent the east. Commerce is represented by a river and steamboat. There is a man plowing in a field to symbolize agriculture. Heading west is a wagon train, and two Native Americans are chasing buffalo. There is a cluster of 34 stars at the top. The state motto appears above this.

Word Definition

MOTTO: a sentence, phrase, or word expressing the spirit or purpose of an organization or group

State Motto

Kansas' state motto is...

Ad Astra per Aspera.
It means
"To the Stars through Difficulties."

Kansas had a state banner prior to adopting the state flag. It was blue silk with a sunflower surrounding the state seal. The word "Kansas" was above that.

Western Meadowlark

The western meadowlark is yellow breasted with a black "V" on its chest. It has brown feathers with white outer tail feathers. The meadowlark is usually about 8.5 inches (22 centimeters) long. This bird has a loud flute-like whistle. The western meadowlark lives in pastures, meadows, and grain fields.

State Tree

State Tree

The Eastern cottonwood is the Kansas state tree. It has an ashy gray bark with long triangular leaves. It can grow from 4–5 feet (1.2–1.5 meters) annually. Their average height is between 75–100 feet (23–30 meters). The cottonwood has brown seeds attached to tufts of cottony hairs. It was one of the few trees that could grow well on the prairie and provided lumber to the pioneers. They used the wood to build cabins, barns, corrals, and churches. It was adopted as the state tree in 1937.

State Flower

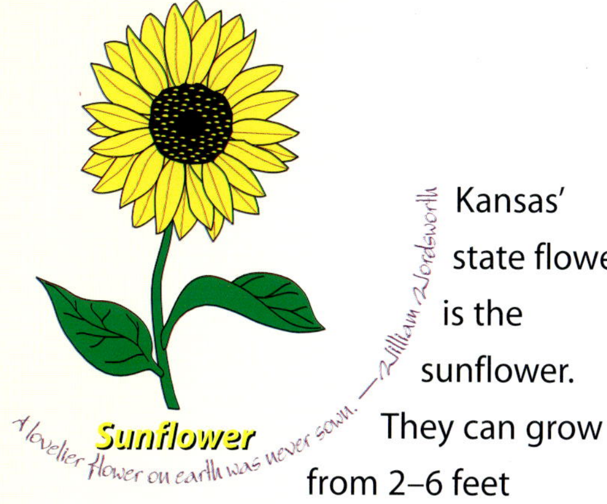

Kansas' state flower is the sunflower. They can grow from 2–6 feet (0.6–1.8 meters) in height. The flowerhead is made up of ray and disk flowers. The disks can be either brown or yellow. The rays are yellow.

RIDDLE:

If the state flower got mixed up with the state bird, what would you have?

ANSWER: A seedless sunflower and one fat bird–it could happen!

BUFFALO

State Animal

The American buffalo was adopted as the state animal in 1955. It is the largest wild animal in America. A bull, male, can be 6 feet (1.8 meters) at the shoulder and 10 feet (3 meters) long. They often weigh over a ton (0.9 metric ton). Bison is another name for buffalo. Great herds of them, as many as 60 million, once roamed over the plains. Native Americans used the buffalo as a source for food, bones, and hides. Today there are several thousand of them thanks to protection given preventing extinction.

Buffalo were killed for sport by the white men who came into Indian lands. By 1885, all that remained of the great western herds was about 75 buffalo.

ORNATE BOX TURTLE

The state reptile is the western box turtle. It was adopted in 1986. Box turtles like to live in dry places. They will burrow into the ground to avoid the heat. They range in size from 4–10 inches (10–25 centimeters). Their shells may have yellow or orange markings. If they get too fat, they may not be able to close their shells. Their diet consists of both plants and animals.

The ornate box turtle has a more colorful top shell than most box turtles.

BARRED TIGER SALAMANDER

State Amphibian

Adopted in 1973, the barred tiger salamander is the state amphibian. Because they like to dig holes, they are often called mole salamanders. They can have stripes that are yellow and black like a tiger. Their length can be from 6–13 inches (15–33 centimeters). It is one of the largest salamanders that lives on land. Mating adults live in ponds with the larvae.

"HOME ON THE RANGE"

"Home on the Range" ("My Western Home") was composed by Brewster Higley and Daniel Kelley. Higley, who wrote the lyrics, was a frontier doctor and homesteader in Smith County. It was originally a poem that was published in The *Pioneer*, a newspaper.

Daniel Kelley put it to music, and it is still a classic learned by school children today.

HARNEY SILT LOAM

State Soil

Harney silt loam is the state soil in Kansas. It was adopted in 1990. It is found in 26 Kansas counties covering an area of 4 million acres (1.6 million hectares). Harney comes from a Wichita Indian word, *harahey*. It means Pawnee people.

A soil by any other name tills not as neat!

The honeybee became the state insect in 1976. It is very important to the success of the crops in Kansas. Farmers are aware of the honeybee's importance for pollinating the plants that produce the crops.

State March

State March

"The Kansas March" was composed by Duff E. Middleton. Kansas' pioneers loved band music; so it is not unusual that they should have a state march. Many of them were all brass bands. During the 19th century, most towns in Kansas had bands. In 1881, the Dodge City Cowboy Band was organized. Some members were cowboys, but most were businessmen from Dodge City. The band became well-known from Texas to the Dakotas. The state march was adopted in 1935.

In 1992, Bill Post composed "Here's Kansas," a newer march for the state of Kansas.

The State of Kansas

Kansas has a rectangular shape.

State Location

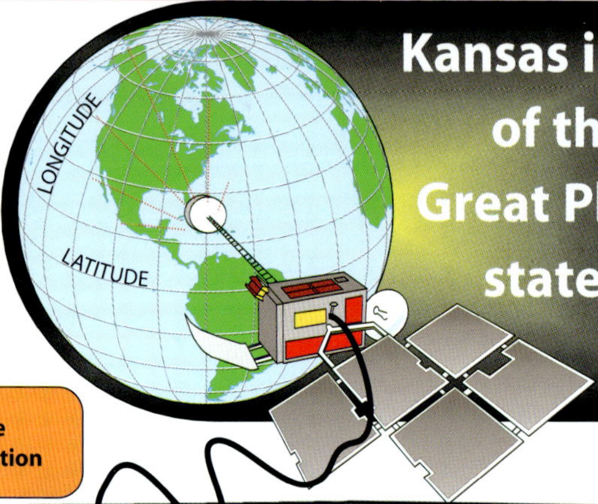

LONGITUDE

LATITUDE

Kansas is one of the Great Plains states.

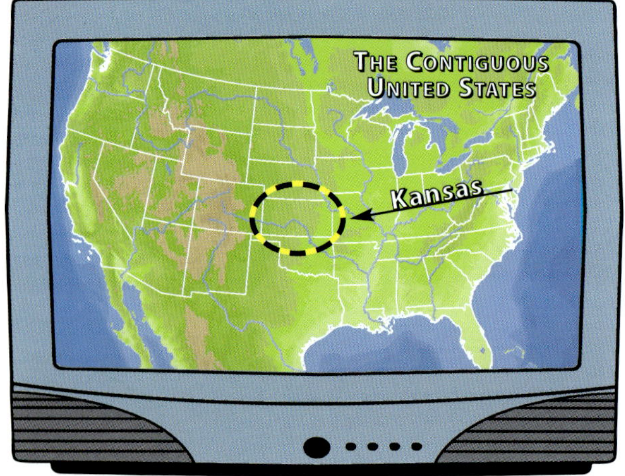

LATITUDE: Imaginary lines which run horizontally east and west around the globe

LONGITUDE: Imaginary lines which run vertically north and south around the globe

On The Border!

These border Kansas:

States:

Colorado
Nebraska
Oklahoma
Missouri

Body of water:

Missouri River

I'll Take the Low Road...

East-West, North-South, Area

Kansas stretches 208 miles (335 kilometers) from north to south—or south to north. Either way, it's a long drive!

Total Area: Approximately 82,282 square miles (213,109 square kilometers)

Land Area: Approximately 81,823 square miles (211,905 square kilometers)

Kansas is 411 miles (661 kilometers) from east to west—or west to east. Either way, it's *still* a long drive!

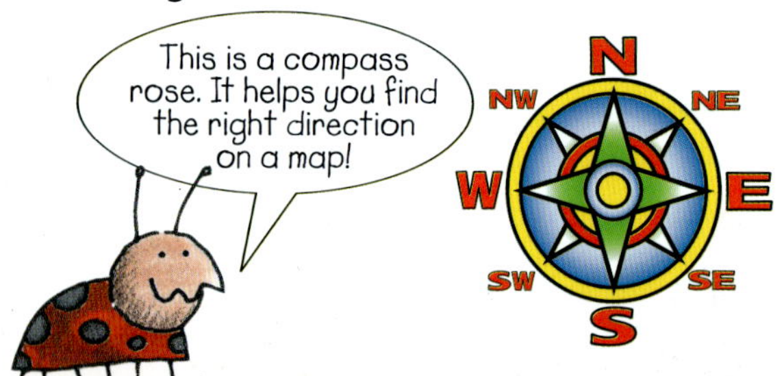

You Take the High Road!

HIGHEST POINT

Mount Sunflower—4,039 feet (1,231 meters)

Mount Sunflower is located in Wallace County on private property. It is open to the public. There is a variety of wildlife including deer, antelope, prairie dogs, and many other birds and animals.

LOWEST POINT

Verdigris River—680 feet (207 meters) above sea level

I'm County-ing on You!

Kansas is divided into 105 counties.

State Counties

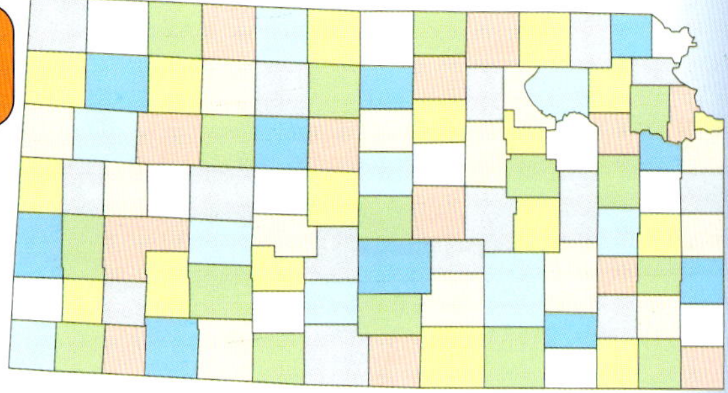

COUNTY: an administrative subdivision of a state or territory

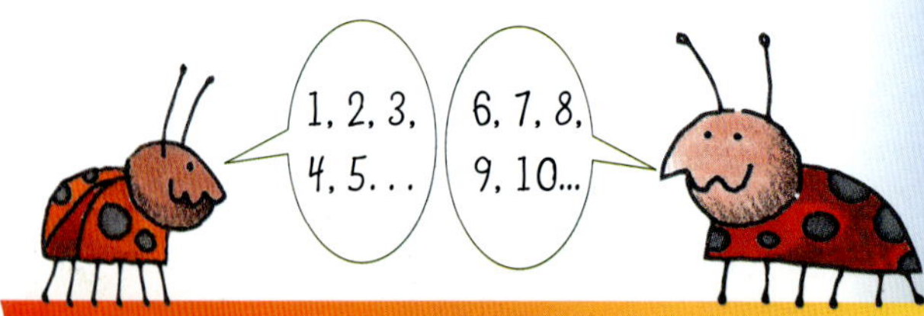

Natural Resources

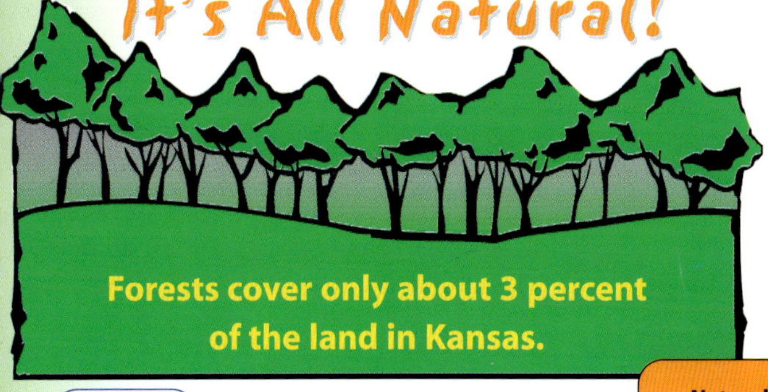

NATURAL RESOURCES: things that exist in or are formed by nature

Rocks and Minerals:

Coal

Lead

Zinc

Stone

Clay Salt

Sand

Gypsum

Weather, Or Not?!

Kansas' temperatures can drop to 30°F (–1°C) in the winter and reach 78°F (26°C) in the summer.

Highest temperature: 121°F (49°C), at Fredonia on July 18, 1936 and near Alton on July 24, 1936

°F=Degrees Fahrenheit °C=Degrees Celsius

Lowest temperature: –40°F (–40°C), at Lebanon on February 13, 1905

Kansas had 2,182 tornadoes reported between 1950 and 1995.

Back On Top

Kansas' topography includes the Central Lowlands which can be divided into the Dissected Till Plains and the Osage Plains on the eastern side of the state. The Great Plains, the Plains Border and High Plains, cover the central and western portion of Kansas.

Sea Level
100 m 328 ft
200 m 656 ft
500 m 1,640 ft
1,000 m 3,281 ft
2,000 m 6,562 ft
5,000 m 16,404 ft

Word Definition

TOPOGRAPHY: the detailed mapping of the features of a small area or district

King of the Hill

Mountains

Sunflower Mountain

Smoky Hill

Geologic Formations

Monument Rocks
(Kansas Pyramids)
Castle Rock

Down The River

Here are some of Kansas' major rivers:

- Kansas River
- Arkansas River
- Cimarron River
- Verdigris River
- Neosho River
- Solomon River
- Republican River
- Marais des Cygnes River
- Smoky Hill River
- Big Blue River

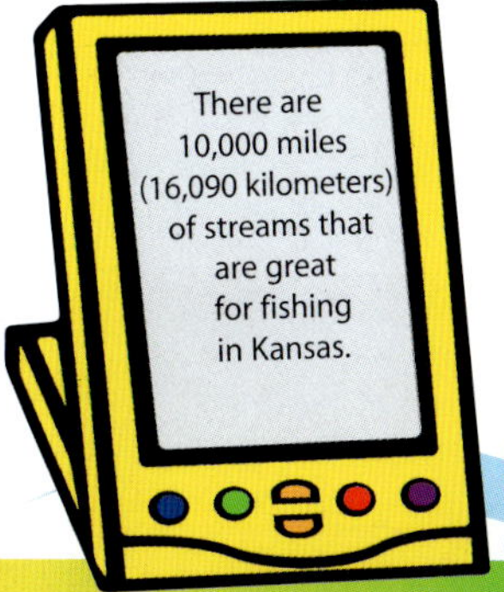

Gone Fishin'

MAJOR LAKES IN KANSAS INCLUDE:

Major Lakes

- Milford Lake
- Turtle Creek Lake

RESERVOIRS

- Cedar Bluff
- Cheney
- Council Grove
- Elk City
- Fall River
- Glen Elder
- John Redmond
- Kanopolis
- Perry
- Turtle Creek
- Webst
- Wilson

Word Definition

RESERVOIR: a body of water stored for public use

ARE YOU A CITY MOUSE... OR A COUNTRY MOUSE?

Have you heard of these wonderful Kansas town, city, or crossroad names? Perhaps you can start your own list!

MAJOR CITIES:

- Wichita
- Kansas City
- Overland Park
- Topeka
- Lawrence
- Olathe
- Leavenworth

UNIQUE NAMES:

- Abilene
- Dodge City
- Liberal
- Ransom
- Protection
- Hiawatha
- Iola
- Emporia

Transportation

Major Interstate Highways

I-70,
I-35 (Kansas Turnpike),
I-135

Railroads

Burlington Northern
Santa Fe Railroad
Union Pacific Railroad

Major Airports

Kansas has an international airport in Kansas City. Other airports include the Wichita Mid-Continent Airport and the Phillip Billard Airport in Topeka.

Navigable Waterways

Missouri River
Kansas River

Timeline

1541 Francisco Vásquez de Coronado, a Spanish explorer, is the first European to visit Kansas

1724 French fur trader Étienne de Bourgmont travels through Kansas

1803 U.S. gets most of Kansas as part of the Louisiana Purchase

1804 Lewis and Clark pass through Kansas on their way to the Pacific

1820 Missouri Compromise prohibits slavery in the land now known as Kansas

1821 William Becknell establishes the Santa Fe Trail that runs mostly through Kansas

1827 Fort Leavenworth becomes the first permanent white settlement in Kansas

1853 Indians living in Kansas have land reclaimed by the U.S. government and are forced to move to Oklahoma

1854 Land opens up to white settlers; beginning of "Bleeding Kansas," fighting between proslavery and antislavery groups moving into Kansas Territory

1861 Kansas enters the Union as the 34th state

1867 U.S. Government negotiates treaty with five Plains Indian Tribes

1874 Grasshoppers invade forcing many new settlers to flee the state

1912 State amendment grants women full suffrage

1934 Dust Bowl devastates Kansas farmers

1952 Kansas native Dwight D. Eisenhower is elected president

1954 U.S. Supreme Court outlaws segregation in schools with the landmark case *Brown vs. Board of Education*

1972 Constitutional amendment increases governor's term from two to four years

1985 Senator Bob Dole of Kansas becomes Senate majority leader

2001 Kansas enters the 21st century

Here come the humans!

Thousands of years ago, ancient peoples inhabited Kansas. They may have originally come across a frozen bridge of land between Asia and Alaska. If so, they slowly traveled east until some settled in what would one day become the state of Kansas.

Some of the early hunters and gatherers left artifacts in this region. They were farmers and eventually settled in villages. They lived in clay or earthen dwellings and built mounds for burial ceremonies.

Early History

These early people were nomadic hunters who traveled in small bands. They camped when seasons offered hunting, fishing, and fruit and nut gathering.

Native Americans Once Ruled!

There were several Native American tribes that lived in the region known as Kansas today. The Kansa lived in the northeast. The Osage could be found further to the south. In the north there were the Pawnee, and in the central part of the state, the Wichita. Using bows and arrows, they hunted buffalo, deer, and antelope. The women gathered nuts and berries and did the farming. They lived in teepees made from animal skins.

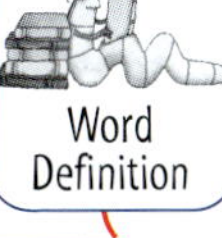

Word Definition

WAMPUM: beads, pierced and strung, used by Indians as money or for ornaments

Land Ho!

In 1541 Spanish explorer Francisco Vásquez de Coronado went in search of gold to a place called Quivira. Near the Kansas River, he and his men met the Wichita Indians. Coronado found no gold or silver; only prunes, nuts, grapes, and mulberries. He returned to Spain in bad favor.

In 1682, René-Robert Cavelier, Sieur de LaSalle, claimed for France all the land that was drained by the Mississippi River. The region was then passed to Spain when France lost a war in 1763, and eventually passed back to France in 1800. In 1803, present-day Kansas became part of what our government acquired with the Louisiana Purchase.

Captain Meriwether Lewis and Lieutenant William Clark trekked through the area on their journey to the Pacific. Lieutenant Zebulon Montgomery Pike crossed the land in 1806. He was on a trip to get the Native Americans to agree to a peace treaty.

Home, Sweet Home

William Becknell, a Missouri trader, established the Santa Fe Trail in 1821 when he used it as a way to travel to the southwest. At that time most of the land in Kansas was used to resettle Indian tribes from east of the Mississippi. The Oregon Trail became the route taken by those wanting to go to the northwest. As people passed through the region many of them ended up settling in Kansas. With the arrival of more settlers to the area, the Native Americans were eventually driven out of Kansas into Oklahoma. Even if the land still belonged to a tribe, it could be taken over by the settlers if they had purchased it. This caused many hostilities between the Indians and the pioneers in the 1800s.

The Santa Fe Trail became an official public road in 1825.

Wheat and Corn!

Kansas is one of the most important states in the nation that grows wheat. About 11 million acres (4,451,700 hectares) of wheat are harvested annually. Kansas produced enough wheat in 1997 to make more than 30 billion loaves of bread.

The first European settlers in Kansas planted corn. Kansans plant 2.7 million acres (1,092,690 hectares) of corn each year. This equals about 386 million bushels of corn! Grain sorghum and soybeans are two other important crops in the state.

WIND WAGONS OF THE WEST!

In 1859 a man by the name of Samuel Peppard and some of his friends developed a case of "gold fever." They wanted to head out to the gold fields. Samuel talked to his friends about using a wind wagon for transportation, but they only laughed at him. As Samuel Peppard worked on constructing one, his friends began to see the possibilities. When it was completed in 1860, Samuel and three others along with 400 pounds (181 kilograms) of provisions headed west. Depending on the wind's strength, they could go as fast as 2 miles (3.2 kilometers) in four minutes. If they made 90 miles (145 kilometers) in one day, that was a good day's travel. They made it as far as Fort Morgan, Colorado, when a whirlwind hit the wagon and tossed it 20 feet (6 meters) into the air. The men were unhurt; however, the wagon was demolished. They got a ride with a baggage train and completed the trip. Peppard and his crew had gone over 500 miles (805 kilometers) before the storm hit. They never discovered any gold but had a golden tale to share with others!

Bleeding

Between 1854 and 1861—just a few years before the Civil War—the border between Kansas and Missouri was the scene of feuds that foreshadowed the larger conflict about to break out nationwide. In 1820 the Missouri Compromise allowed Missouri to enter the Union as a slave state (and Maine as a free state). It also outlawed slavery in territories north of Missouri's border.

By the mid-1850s settlers went to the territories and brought slaves with them. National leaders, including President Franklin Pierce, thought the need to develop a transcontinental railroad might require territories to have more control over their own laws. So the Kansas-Nebraska Act was passed in 1854. The act created the territories of Kansas and Nebraska and allowed each territory to decide the question of slavery in a vote by the people.

Free-state and proslavery groups rivaled for control, hoping to sway the vote. In Linn and Bourbon counties in eastern Kansas, Border Ruffians crossed into Kansas and stuffed ballot boxes (casting fake ballots to sway an election). On May 21, 1856, the Ruffians attacked and burned the town of Lawrence which had been founded by antislavery settlers. To get back at them, abolitionist John Brown dragged five of the proslavery settlers away from their Pottawatomie Creek homesteads and massacred them.

National outrage developed after the massacre near Trading Post. Abolitionist John Brown built a makeshift two-story fort just south of the ravine where the execution occurred.

Kansas

Charles Hamilton, a Georgia proslavery leader, came to the border area and said he would treat all the free-staters as snakes. On May 19, 1858, Hamilton led 20 men into Trading Post, captured 11 unarmed free-staters, and executed them in a ravine. John Greenleaf Whittier memorialized the murdered men in a poem "Le Marais Du Cygne":

On the lintels of Kansas
That blood shall not dry;
Henceforth the Bad Angel
Shall harmless go by;
Henceforth to the sunset,
Unchecked on her way
Shall liberty follow
The march of that day.

After years of border warfare finally ended in 1859, a territorial constitution was passed outlawing slavery, and Kansas entered the Union in January 1861 as a free state—only to see war break out in a divided nation three months later.

Word Definition

ABOLITIONIST: person who believed slavery was wrong and should be ended

Brother

The Civil War was fought between the American states. The argument was over states' rights to make their own decisions, including whether or not to own slaves. Some of the southern states began to secede (leave) the Union. They formed the Confederate States of America.

The Civil War

Kansas contributed troops to the Union cause during the war. Two-thirds of the male population (20,000 men) joined the Union effort. Both Native and African-Americans marched with other Union troops raised in Kansas. During the battle of Mine Creek forces drove Confederate troops back to Missouri in the only significant Civil War battle fought in Kansas. However, William Quantrill and his Confederate guerrillas would raid communities in eastern Kansas until the end of the war.

The Civil War was also called the War Between the States. Soldiers often found themselves fighting against former friends and neighbors, even brother against brother. Those who did survive often went home without an arm, leg, or both, since amputation was the "cure" for most battlefield wounds. More Americans were killed during the Civil War than during World Wars I and II together!

In 1863, the Emancipation Proclamation, given by U.S. President Abraham Lincoln, freed the slaves still under Confederate control. Some slaves became sharecroppers; others went to Northern states to work in factories.

Get It In Writing!

1776
Declaration of Independence

1789
U.S. Constitution

1820
Missouri Compromise

1830
Indian Removal Bill

1854
Kansas-Nebraska Act

1859
State Constitution

1862
Homestead Acts

1954
Brown v. Board of Education

Welcome To America!

People have come to Kansas from other states and many other countries on almost every continent! As time goes by, Kansas' population grows more diverse. This means that people of different races and from different cultures and ethnic backgrounds have moved to Kansas.

In the past, many immigrants have come to Kansas from Germany, Russia, Britain, Switzerland, Belgium, France, Sweden, and from Norway. More recently, people have migrated to Kansas from Hispanic countries such as Mexico or from Southeast Asian countries. Only a certain number of immigrants are allowed to move to America each year. Many of these immigrants eventually become U.S. citizens.

1874

Grasshoppers swarm and create destruction

1886

Blizzard destroys some of the state's cattle herds

1903

Smoky Hill Flood kills 415 people

1916–1918

Codell has deadly tornadoes three years in a row on May 20

1930

Dust Bowl Storms destroy farms and erode the soil

1955

Udall tornado kills 80 people

1991

Andover tornado kills 18 people; injures 200

Legal Stuff

1853

U.S. government reclaims land from the Native Americans that was to be theirs forever

1867

Government negotiates treaty with five Plains tribes

1880

Kansas becomes first state to have constitutional prohibition

1887

Women have voting rights in municipal elections

1937

Kansas establishes a state department of social welfare

1958

Kansas approves a right-to-work law

1965

State legislature provides a system of junior colleges

Pilot

Amelia Earhart was the first woman to make a solo flight across the Atlantic Ocean in 1932.

Author

Laura Ingalls Wilder wrote a series of nine novels. *Little House on the Prairie* describes her experiences while living in Kansas.

Survivors

Nancy and Julia German, five and seven years of age, were captured by the Cheyenne in 1874 when their family was attacked while heading west. The squaw in charge of their care left them on the plains. Eventually troops were sent out to find them. The Indians had come back, and there was a battle. The girls were rescued. Their two older sisters who had also been taken were not saved until 1875. They were the only survivors from their family of nine.

Fight! Fight! Fight!

Wars that Kansans participated in:

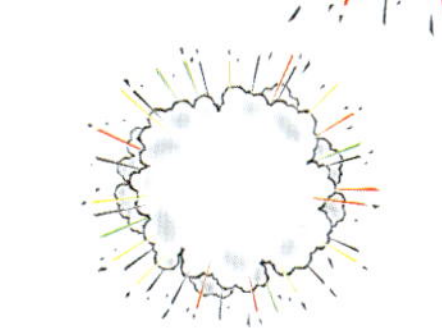

- **Border War**
- **Civil War**
- **Spanish-American War**
- **World War I**
- **World War II**
- **Korean War**
- **Vietnam War**
- **Persian Gulf War**

Awesome Airplanes

With Flying Colors!

Kansas has four major aircraft companies. Boeing Company has become the largest aerospace company in the world. They are the largest manufacturer of commercial jetliners, military aircraft, and the countries largest contractor for NASA. Cessna Aircraft is located in Independence. They are the biggest producer of general aviation aircraft. Learjet Inc. makes corporate jets. Raytheon Aircraft Company makes Beech aircraft and special-mission aircraft for the U.S. Government and other nations. They also produce electronic and computer systems that are related to aviation.

Flight Facts

- Henry Call of Girard manufactured the first Kansas airplane.
- The first helicopter was patented in 1910 in Goodland by William Purvis.
- Claude Ryan from Parsons designed and built the *Spirit of St. Louis* flown by Charles Lindbergh.

Indian Tribes

Comanche
Kiowa
Cheyenne
Arapaho

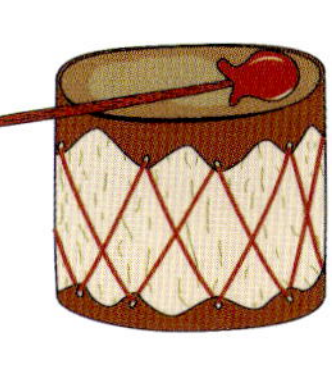

These Native Americans were some of the best riders in North America. Their skill on horseback was remarkable.

The Spanish who brought horses into the region changed the Indians lifestyle. With the advent of the horse, Comanche, Kiowa, Cheyenne, and Arapaho Indians moved into western Kansas. They followed the buffalo herds moving from place to place. Indian wars would break out when tribes wanted to occupy the same land. The Comanche were fierce warriors.

The Indians of Kansas could not have known that the coming of the white man would mean an end to the way of life they had known for hundreds of years.

Here, There, Everywhere!

The **Homestead Act of 1862** gave a settler 160 acres (65 hectares) of land for a small price.

The settler had to work the land for five years. Due to a lack of water and other conditions, many farmers could not make a go of it. Some sold up their land cheaply and moved to other places.

For those who stayed on, life was not easy. The shortage of wood on the prairie led them to build houses out of sod—hardened grass and dirt. For this reason they were called sodbusters! They endured many hardships like the plague of grasshoppers and droughts. Water was scarce and they often walked a mile (1.6 kilometers) to get to a stream. Dried sticks, weeds, and dung from buffalo and cattle were used to heat their homes. For the pioneers, life was never easy on the prairie.

State Founders

Founding Fathers

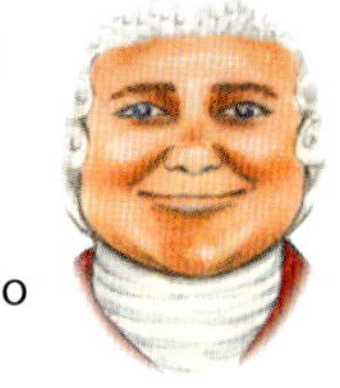

Seth M. Hays—Indian trader; started a trading post at Council Grove to provide supplies for those traveling west; believed to be first white settler in area

Edmund Gibson Ross—led free-staters to Kansas; became U.S. senator from Kansas in 1866

Joseph McCoy—rancher; brought first cattle herds to Abilene for shipment north; helped Abilene become an important cow town

Dr. Charles Robinson—member of the New England Emigrant Aid Society; brought many immigrants to settle in Kansas; after statehood he became the first governor

Founding Mothers

Carry Nation—temperance leader; carried a hatchet to destroy saloons in Kansas in her crusade against alcoholic beverages

Lucy Hobbs Taylor—came to Kansas to practice dentistry; first woman dentist in the U.S.

Mary Lease—orator; worked toward forming the Populist Party, a national political party

Sara Robinson—writer; her book, *Kansas, Its Interior and Exterior Life*, encouraged many to come to Kansas

Buffalo Soldiers—African-Americans who served on the frontier to keep the peace; Indians called them this because of their bravery and curly hair

Eva Jesseye—called the "female dean of black music" in America; singer, composer, and arranger of spirituals

Gwendolyn Brooks—poet; described the plight of blacks in her verses; won Pulitzer prize in poetry in 1950

Gale Sayers—professional football player; considered one of the National Football League's greatest running backs

Elwood "Bingo" De Moss—professional baseball player; starred for the Negro League baseball teams; considered to be the greatest second baseman of his time

Lutie Lytle—first African-American female licensed attorney in the U.S.; first female attorney to appear before the U.S. Supreme Court

Benjamin "Pap" Singleton—formed a company that helped hundreds of former slaves move to Kansas; known as the Father of the Exodus

DID SOMEONE SAY BOO!?

THE INTERIOR DESIGNER GHOST

There is a house in Atchison that was purchased along with the furnishings. The new owners decided to make a few changes. After taking down one painting and wrapping it up to be put away, they discovered it rehung on the wall the next day. When they attempted more than once to hang a clock on the wall of the dining room, they would find it in the middle of the floor. They finally gave up on the clock. Obviously, their ghost's tastes are of a different decorating style!

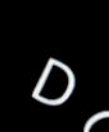

DO YOU BELIEVE IN GHOSTS?

Sports Stuff

- **Wilt Chamberlain**—professional basketball player; one of the greatest scorers in NBA history; played for the Philadelphia 76ers and the Los Angeles Lakers
- **George Brett**—baseball player; played for the Kansas City Royals; one of Kansas' baseball legends
- **Walter "Big Train" Johnson**—professional baseball player; considered to be one of the greatest pitchers of all time; played for the Washington Senators
- **Ronald Kramer**—professional football player; tight end for the Green Bay Packers under Vince Lombardi
- **Rick Mears**—race car driver; won Indianapolis 500 four times
- **Tom Watson**—golfer; learned to play at Shawnee Mission
- **Joseph Bert Tinker**—professional baseball player; shortstop for the Chicago Cubs; elected to Baseball Hall of Fame in 1946
- **Tara Knott**—weightlifter; took the gold in Sydney Olympics 2000
- **Christi Ambrosi**—softball outfielder; team won the gold at the 2000 Olympics
- **Marilyn Smith**—golfer; won 22 tournaments in the Ladies Professional Golf Association circuit
- **Barry Sanders**—won the 1988 Heisman trophy; has played for the Detroit Lions

Entertainers

William Inge— novelist and playwright; won 1953 pulitzer prize in drama for *Picnic*

Emmett Kelly—clown who worked for Ringling Brother, Barnum and Bailey Circus; created character "Weary Willie"

Dennis Hopper—actor and director; starred in *Rebel Without a Cause*; wrote and directed *Easy Rider*

Buster Keaton—stone-faced comedian; starred in silent films

Stan Kenton—jazz musician; combined jazz with Afro-Cuban rhythms

Hattie McDaniel—won Academy Award for supporting actress in her role as Mammy in *Gone With the Wind*

Zasu Pitts—actress who played flighty roles as friends to leading ladies

Charles Buddy Rogers—actor who starred in *Wings*

Vivian Vance—actress who played Lucille Ball's friend in the *I Love Lucy* television series

Marvin Rainwater—country singer; performed in Native American dress; recorded "Gonna Find Me a Bluebird"

Samuel Ramey—one of the most popular opera stars; most recorded bass in history

Authors

- **Dorothy Cannfield Fisher**—novelist; explored the lives of middle-class women in her books
- **Edgar Watson Howe**—publisher and novelist; editor of the *Atchison Globe*, a powerful force in Kansas politics
- **Edgar Lee Masters**—poet; wrote *Spoon River Anthology*
- **Damon Runyan**—author; wrote *Guys and Dolls, Blue Plate Special,* and *Take It Easy*
- **Paul Wellman**—author and reporter; wrote 23 books and some screenplays
- **William Allen White**—writer, editor, and publisher; won two Pulitzer Prizes for his editorials and his autobiography
- **Sara Paretsky**—author of detective novels; V. I. Warshawski is the main character for her best-sellers
- **William Least Heat-Moon**—author of epic, *PrairyErth*; has made Chase County well-known throughout the world
- **L. Frank Baum**—author of *The Wizard of Oz* which later went on to become a famous movie loved by children of all ages
- **William Gibson**—author of *The Miracle Worker*, based on Helen Keller's life

Ernest Hemingway lived in Kansas while he was writing *A Farewell to Arms* which was published in 1929.

Artists

Stan Herd—combines farming skills with art to create crop art; by planting seeds on huge canvasses of farmland he designs portraits; his work has appeared on national magazine covers

John Steuart Curry—mural painter whose works appear at the state capitol; he has also sculpted buffalo and Native Americans on horseback

Mort Walker—cartoonist; created comic strips *Beetle Bailey* and *Hi and Lois*

Rudolph Wendelen—drew Smokey Bear, the mascot of the U.S. Forest Service

Robert Merrell Gage—sculptor; created *Pioneer Woman of Kansas*

Gordon Alexander Buchanan Parks—photographer; won awards as photographer for *Life* magazine

Sven Birger Sandzen—painted prairie scenes using an impressionistic technique

Frederic Remington—artist; while he owned a sheep ranch in Kansas, he did early sketches of life in the west

RIDDLE:
What are the famous words Smokey Bear is known for saying?

ANSWER:
Only YOU can prevent forest fires!

Very Important People

Walter Percy Chrysler—industrialist; established Chrysler Corporation, became the third largest automotive company in the country

William "Buffalo Bill" Cody—scout for the U.S. Army and led buffalo

hunting expeditions; Pony Express Rider; scout for Kansas cavalry against the Indians; organized and starred in famous Wild West show that toured the nation and Europe

Cyrus Holliday—industrialist; founded the Atchison, Topeka, & Santa Fe Railroad

Charles, Karl, and William Menninger—psychiatrists; founded the Menninger Foundation, a leading psychiatric center

Clyde Tombaugh—astronomer; in 1930, discovered the planet Pluto

Samuel Crumbine—secretary of the state board of health; crusaded against improper labeling of drugs, food and water contamination, sharing drinking cups, and other unsanitary habits

More Very Important People

Dan and Frank Carney—founders of Pizza Hut restaurants; started first business for $600 in a rented building in Wichita; after merging with PepsiCo, more than 10,000 Pizza Huts can be found around the world

Ron Evans—commander of pilot ship during *Apollo 17* flight to the moon

Clyde Vernon Cessna—designed and built his own airplanes; joined with Beech to form Travel Air Manufacturing Company; went on to form Cessna Aircraft Company

Joe Engle—astronaut; flew on the maiden voyage of the space shuttle *Columbia*

Steve Hawley—astronaut; carried Kansas flags on first flight of space shuttle *Discovery*

Colonel Henry Leavenworth—started the first white settlement at Fort Leavenworth in what would eventually become Kansas

Political Leaders

Clark Adams Clifford—U.S. secretary of defense under President Lyndon Johnson

Charles Curtis—U.S. representative; Senate majority leader; U.S. vice-president under President Hoover; only person of Indian descent to hold this office

Robert Joseph Dole—U.S. representative from Kansas; U.S. senator; ran for president of the U.S. in 1996 on the Republican ticket

Dwight David Eisenhower—supreme commander of Allied forces in Europe during WWII; became the 34th president of the U.S.

Milton Eisenhower—headed Office of War Information during WWII; became president of three different universities over the years

Georgia Neese Clark Gray—public official; U.S. treasurer

Nancy Landon Kassebaum—first woman U.S. senator from Kansas

Alfred Mossman (Alf) Landon—governor of Kansas; lost the 1936 presidential election to Franklin D. Roosevelt

Susanna M. Salter—first woman mayor to be elected in the U.S. in 1887; mayor of Argonia

Minnie Grinstead—first woman elected to the Kansas legislature

GOOD GUYS

William Barclay (Bat) Masterson—law officer; scout; fought against the Indians; gambler; Sheriff of Ford County; believed in upholding the law and keeping the peace; liked to wear fancy clothes and carry a cane

Wyatt Earp—law officer; responsible for keeping the peace in Kansas cattle towns

James Butler "Wild Bill" Hickok—stage coach driver, guerilla fighter and scout for General Custer; U.S. marshal in Abilene

BAD DUDES

The Dalton Gang (Bob, Emmet, and Gratton)—attempted to rob two banks in their hometown of Coffeyville; the town learned of the plan and met the gang with gunfire; Emmett survived and served 15 years in prison; the two other brothers and their two hired guns were killed

CHURCHES
Keeping the Faith

Cathedral of the Plains, Victoria—built of native limestone in 1911

Beecher Bible and Rifle Church, Wabaunsee—antislavery Congregationalist church built in 1862; Bibles and rifles are on display

Old Stone Church, Osawatomie—built in 1861 to serve the Reverend Samuel L. Adair's congregation; the kind-hearted abolitionist was John Brown's brother-in-law

St. Benedict's Abbey, Atchison—Tudor Gothic structure; built from 1927–1929 out of Waverly Ledge limestone

Iowa, Sac, and Fox Presbyterian Mission, Highland—built in 1846 to serve the Native Americans and white settlers

SCHOOLS

University of Kansas, Lawrence

Kansas State University, Manhattan

Wichita State University

Emporia State University

Fort Hays State University

Pittsburg State University

Baker University, Baldwin City

Benedictine College, Atchison

Bethany College, Lindsborg

Marymount College, Salina

University of Topeka

U.S. Army Command and General Staff College, Fort Leavenworth

Historic Sites

Barton County Historical Village and Museum, Great Bend—settlement from the late 1800s–1900s

El Cuartelejo, Scott City—Picuris tribe pueblo; occupied by them from 1650–1720

Historic Front Street, Dodge—re-creation of two blocks of what the street looked like in the 1870s; museum of the Old West

Shawnee Indian Mission, Kansas City—used as an Indian school from 1830–1862

Cedar Crest Governor's Mansion, Topeka—built in 1928; Norman-style chateau; home to Kansas' chief official

Gallery of Also Rans, Norton—unsuccessful presidential candidates are honored here

Huron Indian Cemetery, Kansas City—Wyandot tribe's burial ground between 1844 and 1959

Little House on the Prairie, near Independence—an exact copy of the log cabin on the plains lived in by author Laura Ingalls Wilder

Mid-America All Indian Center and Museum, Wichita—exhibits of Native American cultures spanning the Plains, Southwest, Northwest, and Eskimo areas of settlement

Old Abilene Town—reproduction of Abilene during the cattle boom

Historical Homes

- **Amelia Earhart Birthplace**, Atchison—built in 1861
- **Fred Harvey House**, Leavenworth—built in 1875 of limestone ashlar; owned by man who built restaurants all along the Sante Fe Railroad
- **Jesse A. Hoel Residence**, Kansas City—finest domestic architecture in the city

- **Grinter House**, Kansas City—constructed in 1829; Grinter started up the first ferry service across the Kansas River in 1831
- **Mahaffie Farmstead**, Olathe—two-story stone house owned by the man who had the biggest livestock herd in the area; used as a stagecoach stop on the Sante Fe Trail
- **George Innes House**, Lawrence—three-story Queen Anne-style building; built in 1889 by Innes, a leading dry-goods merchant
- **Warkentin House**, Newton—built in 1887 by a Russian immigrant who aided the settlement of Mennonites in Kansas
- **Carry Nation Home**, Medicine Lodge—furnishings and memorabilia from the days of her involvement in the temperance movement

A few of Kansas' famous Battles

- **Battle of Mine Creek**, Linn County—in 1864 in the only major Civil War batle fought in Kansas Confederate forces entered Kansas and were turned away by Union forces who drove them back to Missouri
- **Last Indian Raid**, Lawrence—in 1878, Chief Dull Knife and a group of Northen Cheyenne wanted to cross Kansas and go back to their home in Montana; they attacked many of the settlers; 41 were killed; many of the Indians were captured in Nebraska and Montana

A few of Kansas' famous Forts

- **Fort Hays**—constructed in 1865 to protect military roads, guard the mails, and to defend the men working on the Union Pacific Railroad

Fort Larned National Historic Site—built in 1859 to protect travelers along the Santa Fe Trail

Fort Leavenworth—active military post built in 1827; oldest post in continuous operation west of the Mississippi River

Fort Riley, Junction City—home of the U.S. Calvary; General George Custer's home is on the grounds; first territorial capital

Fort Scott National Historic Site—1842 military post; maintained to keep peace on the Indian frontier

Libraries

Check out the following special Kansas libraries! (Do you have a library card? Have you worn it out yet?!)

Watson Memorial Library, Lawrence—located at the University of Kansas; largest library in the state

Vinland Library—first library to open in Kansas in 1859

Kansas State Historical Society Library, Topeka—collections of history on Native Americans; one of the largest newspaper collections in the country

Emporia Library—collection of city directories; newspapers from 1857; complete file of Emporia Gazette

Dwight D. Eisenhower Library, Abilene—houses presidential memorabilia and papers

Baker University Library, Baldwin City—houses Bishop William A. Quayle Bible collection

Zoos and Attractions

Bartlett Arboretum, Belle Plaine—flowers, ornamental grasses, shrubs, and trees from around the world

International Forest of Friendship, Atchison—contains trees from all 50 states and 33 countries

The Kansas Cosmosphere and Space Center, Hutchinson—one of nation's most important space centers

Omnisphere and Science Center, Wichita—planetarium and hands-on science center

Fick Fossil and History Museum, Oakley—fossils, rocks, minerals, and shark-tooth collection; sod house and replica of train depot

Safari Zoological Park, Caney—100 different species of animals; including big cats, monkeys, llamas, and snakes

Kansas University Natural History Museum, Lawrence—General George Custer's horse, Comanche, is on display; a wonderful fossil collection, and many mounted animals in their natural habitats

Maxwell Wildlife Refuge, Flint Hills—buffalo and elk roam free; experience the prairie as the pioneers did

The Tall Grass Prairie National Preserve, Cottonwood Falls—10, 894 acre (4,409 hectare) prairie preserve; mammals, plants, birds, reptiles, and amphibians

Kansas Museum of History, Topeka—thousands of exhibits concerning the history of Kansas

Coronado Museum, Liberal—traces the history of Spanish explorer's routes through the state

High Plains Museum, Goodland—Native American artifacts, farm machinery, and household items

Museum of Anthropology, Lawrence—artifacts from the Americas, Africa, Australia, and New Guinea at the University of Kansas

The University of Kansas Natural History Museum, Lawrence—state's largest natural history museum; located at the University of Kansas

Snow Entomological Museum, Lawrence—University of Kansas insect exhibit

Pawnee Indian Village Museum, Belleville—built near the site of a Pawnee Village; learn of this tribe's culture

Lest We Forget

Buffalo Soldiers Monument, Leavenworth—honors 9th and 10th Cavalries made up of African-American soldiers when the Army was segregated

Dwight D. Eisenhower Center, Abilene—museum honoring the life of President Eisenhower and his family

Sarah Davis Memorial, Hiawatha—built by her husband at the time of her death in 1930; life-size Italian statues depicting scenes from their life together until the time of his death; located in Mount Hope Cemetery

Memorial Rose Garden, Riverside Park—more than 80 varieties of roses to honor those who have died for our country; usually bloom near Memorial Day

The Kansas Teacher Hall of Fame, Dodge—honors state's teachers and also has a museum of early classroom items

The Arts

Helen F. Spencer Museum of Art, Lawrence—University of Kansas; has the most extensive collection of art in the state

Lawrence Art Center—displays the works of local artists

Wichita Art Museum—American art from colonial times to the present; and works of "cowboy artist" Charles M. Russell

Sagebrush Gallery of Western Art, Medicine Lodge—exhibits of western painting and sculptures

Edwin A. Ulrich Museum of Art, Wichita —fine art museum at Wichita State University

Birger Sandzen Memorial Gallery, Lindsborg—celebrates the works of Kansas artist Birger Sandzen

To be, or not to be involved in the arts–that is the question. What is your answer?

The Pony Express

Pony Express Riders began riding in 1860. They traveled a route between St. Joseph, Missouri, and San Francisco, California, carrying the mail. A rider had to travel 75–100 miles (121–161 kilometers) without stopping except to change horses. The pay was $50 a month along with room and board. Young men, 18–20 years old, were wanted who weighed no more than 125 pounds (56 kilograms). They had to be loyal and fearless and able to face the dangers along the trail.

The Pony Express only lasted 18 months. It was put out of business by the transcontinental telegraph. William Cody rode for a short time for the Pony Express when he was a young man. A statue in Marysville honors the Pony Express riders.

Roads, Bridges, and More!

Roads,

Pancake Boulevard, Liberal—Highway 54; International Pancake Race held here; contestants flip a large pancake in a skillet at beginning of race; run 0.25 mile (400 meters); flip the pancake again at end; first to complete this race wins

Old Route 66—cuts through the corner of Kansas from Galena to Riverton

Santa Fe Trail—opened in 1821; Osage chiefs sold the right-of-way for $800; used by pioneers and gold-seekers heading West

Chisholm Trail—opened the way for railheads in Kansas; great herds of cattle were moved north through Kansas headed to market

Bridges,

The Bow String Bridge, Meriden—100-year-old iron structure spanning Rock Creek

Stone Arch Bridges, Emporia—Chase County rock has been used to build them; 1886 bridge is still standing

Theorosa's Bridge, Valley Center—crosses Jester Creek; supposedly named for a young girl who disappeared there in the 1800s

and More!

Smoky River Canoe Trail, Kanopolis—10.5 miles (16.9 kilometers) long; 4–5 hours to complete

Topeka Trolleys—scenic tours of the historic section of the city

Kansas Quilt Walk, Great Bend—seven historic quilt patterns built into the sidewalks along the square

Swamps and Caverns

Swamps

Cheyenne Bottoms Wildlife Area, Great Bend—makes up 19,000 acres (7,689 hectares) of wetlands; marshy swampland that attracts many varieties of water fowl and migratory birds

Jamestown State Waterfowl Management Area—large salt lake marsh; habitat for birds and other wildlife; one of a series of wetlands

Caverns

Palmer Cave, Ellsworth County—contains ancient Indian drawings on stone

Comanche County Caves—128 caves; often shelter large populations of bats

Sink holes—found in various areas of state usually where underground mining has taken place; 300 sink holes exist in Kansas where the roofs of underground caves have collapsed

Question:
- Which is the stalagmite?
- Which is the stalactite?

Answer: Stalactites are long, tapering formations hanging from the roof of a cavern, produced by continuous watery deposits containing certain minerals. The mineral-rich water dripping from stalactites often forms conical stalagmites on the floor below.

Word Definition

SPELUNKER: a person who goes exploring caves for fun

Kansas' Animals include:

Buffalo
Deer
Elk
Coyote
Muskrat
Opossum
Prairie dog
Rabbit
Raccoon
Bear
Skunk
Mink
Rattlesnakes
Beaver
Badger
Fox

Prairie dogs like to live in large colonies marked by low mounds of dirt and sand. The mounds are created from the burrows they have dug underground. They feed mainly on grass and other plants.

Take a Walk on the Wild Side!

Some endangered Kansas animals are:

Gray bat
Indiana bat
Whooping crane
Eskimo curlew
Bald eagle
Black-footed ferret
Neosho madtom
Piping plover
Arkansas River shiner
Topeka shiner
Pallid sturgeon
Least tern
Black-capped vireo

The black-footed ferret is the largest true weasel. It can grow up to 18 inches (46 centimeters) with a 6-inch (15-centimeter) tail. It has black feet and a black band across its eyes.

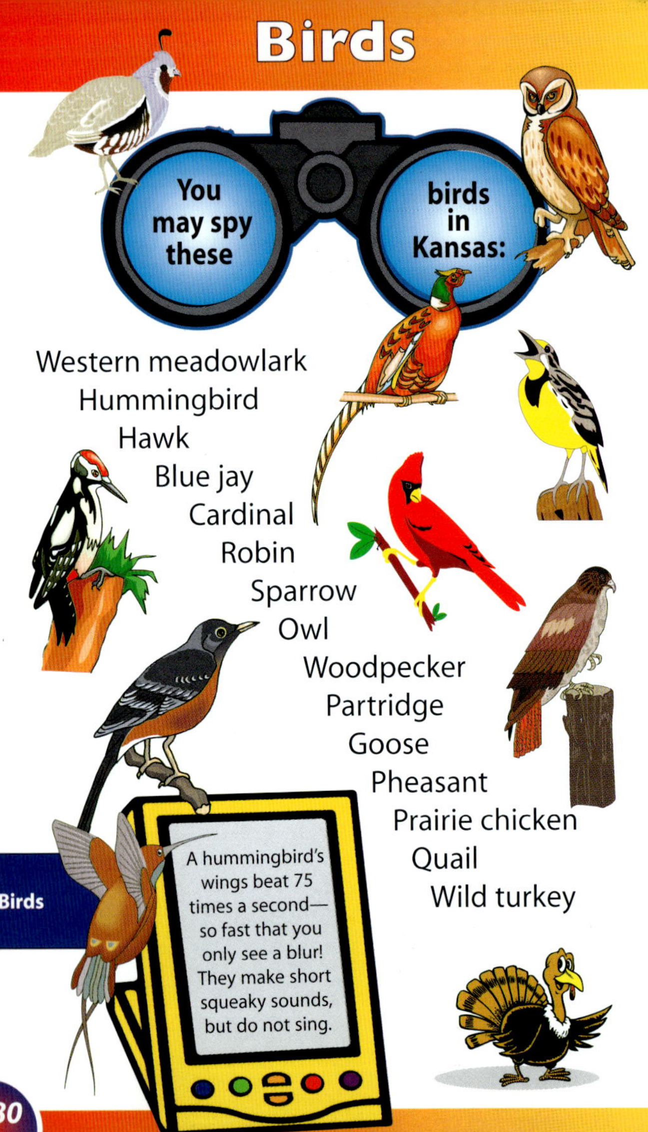

Western meadowlark
Hummingbird
Hawk
Blue jay
Cardinal
Robin
Sparrow
Owl
Woodpecker
Partridge
Goose
Pheasant
Prairie chicken
Quail
Wild turkey

A hummingbird's wings beat 75 times a second—so fast that you only see a blur! They make short squeaky sounds, but do not sing.

Don't let these Kansas bugs bug you!

Whirligig beetle
Chinch bug
Codling moth
Milkweed bug
Treehopper
Lacewing
Cabbage butterfly
Mole cricket
Walking stick
Buckeye

Honeybee

Viceroy butterfly

Grasshopper

Ladybug

Whirligig beetles have two pairs of eyes–one pair looks above the water, the other under it!

Swimming in Kansas' waters:

- Bass
- Bluegill
- Catfish
- Crappie
- Carp
- Walleye

Pond Critters

In Kansas' ponds, you may find:

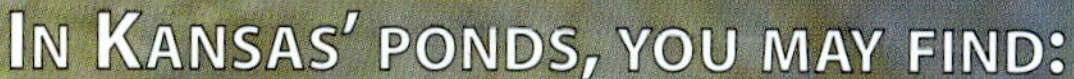

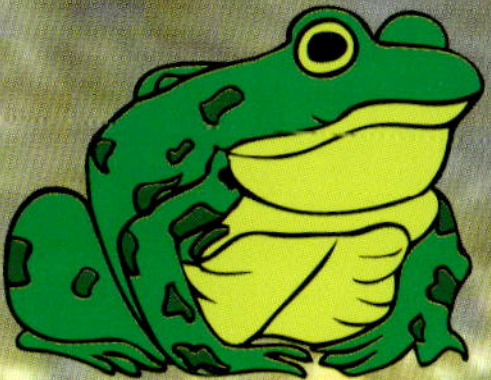

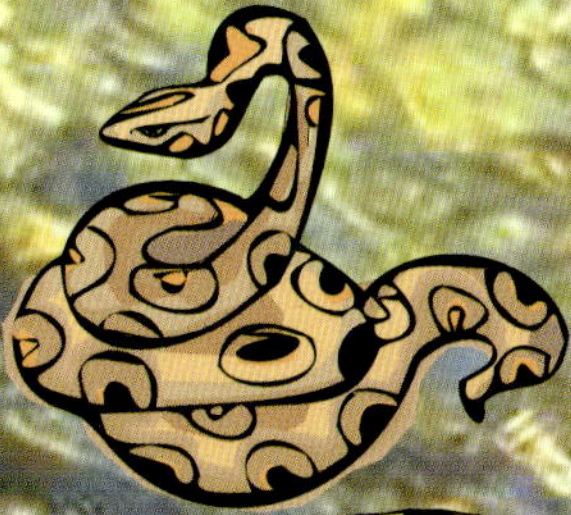

Bull frog

Leopard frog

Toad

Tiger salamander

Pickerel frog

Spadefoot

Water snake

Western cottonmouth water moccasin

Alligator snapping turtle

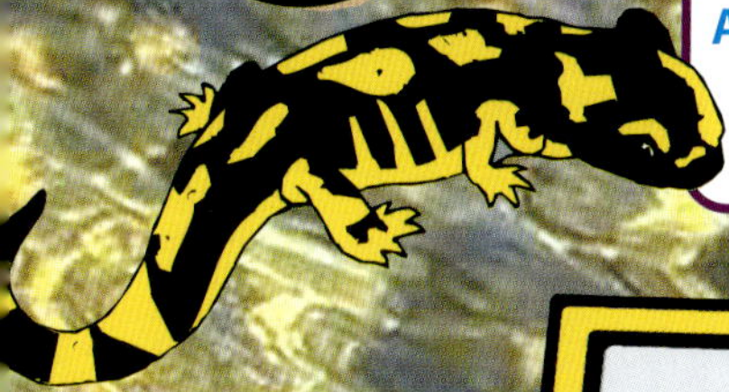

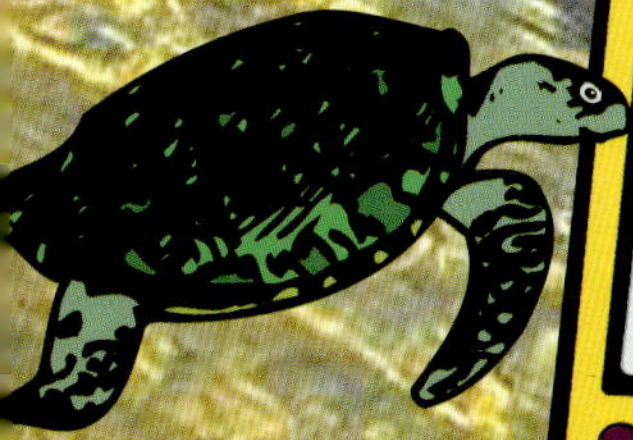

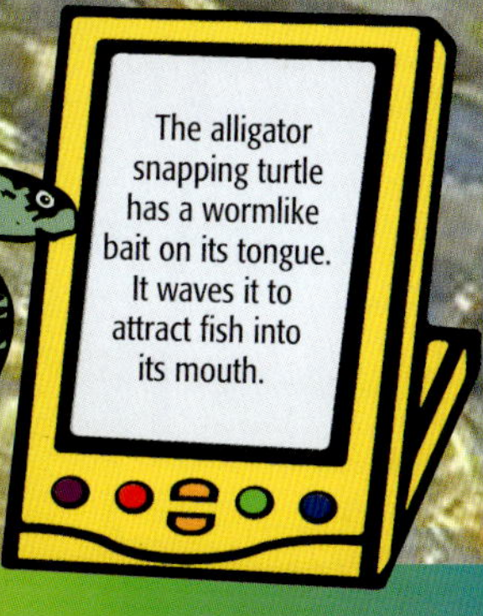
The alligator snapping turtle has a wormlike bait on its tongue. It waves it to attract fish into its mouth.

Kansas Rocks!

Castle Rock, Grove County—70-foot (21-meter) high chalk spire; natural landmark shaped by centuries of whistling wind

Monument Rocks National Landmark, Smoky Hill River—chalky bluffs and pyramids; many fossils especially of pterosaurs discovered in this region by archaeologists

Rock City, Minneapolis—huge sandstone boulders; some 27 feet (8.2 meters) in diameter

Post Rock County has miles and miles of stone fence posts. This area has a large stone quarry which is where they extract the fence posts.

TREEMENDOUS!

THESE TREES TOWER OVER KANSAS:

EASTERN COTTONWOOD
ASH
BLACK WALNUT
PECAN
HICKORY
ELM
HACKBERRY
SYCAMORE
WILLOW
MAPLE
OAK
DOGWOOD
LOCUST
RED CEDAR
BOX ELDER

Wildflowers

Are you crazy about these Kansas wildflowers?

Tumbleweed
Sunflower
Aster
Clover
Ragwort
Columbine
Daisy
Goldenrod

Thistle
Morning glory
Osage orange
Prairie phlox
Prickly pear
Yucca
May apple
Wild indigo

Cream of the Crops

Agricultural products from Kansas:

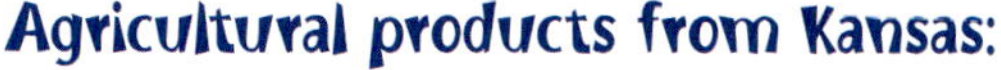

Wheat
Sorghum
Oats
Soybeans
Sugar beets
Rye
Barley

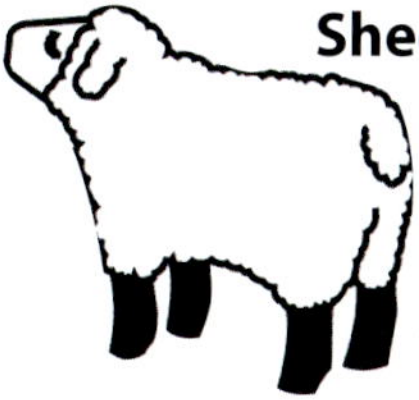

Sheep

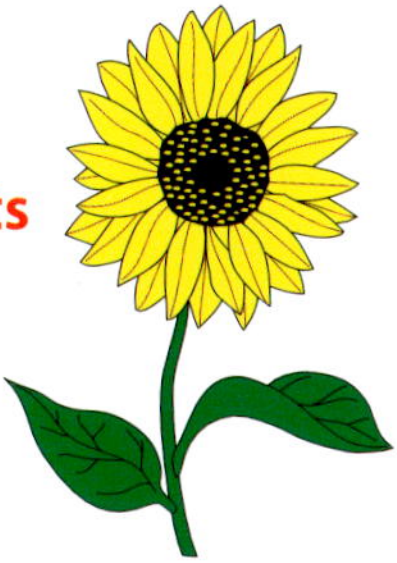

Sunflowers

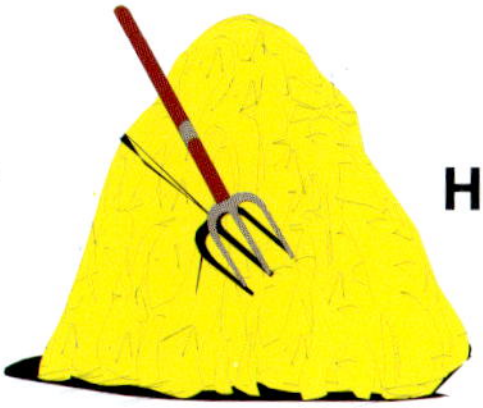

Hay

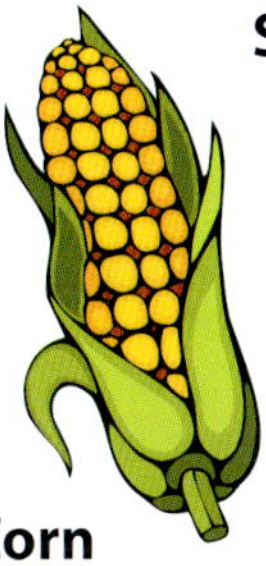

Corn

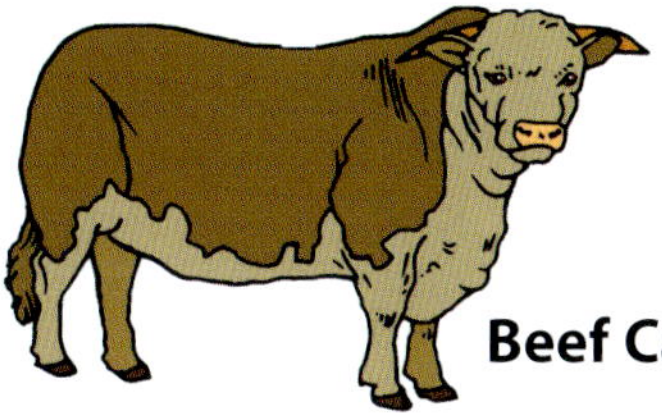

Beef Cattle

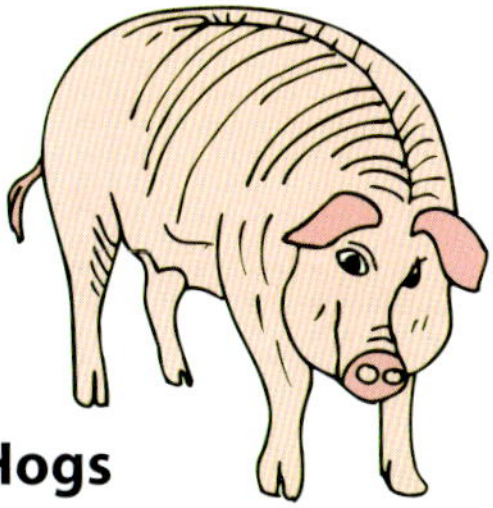

Hogs

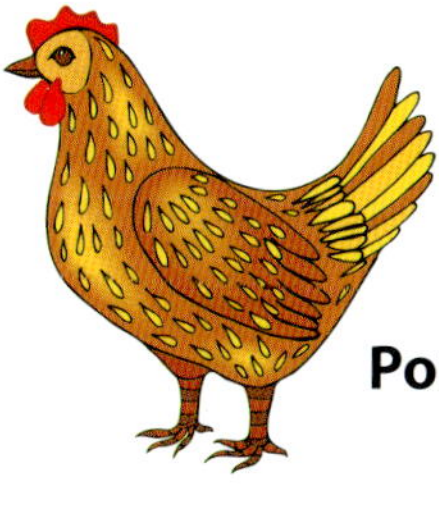

Poultry

First/Big/Small/Etc.

A **ball of twine** in Cawker City measures over 38 feet (11.6 meters) in circumference and is still growing.

Hutchinson has a grain elevator that is 0.5-mile (0.8-kilometer) long and holds **46 million bushels of grain.**

Dodge City is the **windiest city in the U.S.**

Ice cream and cherry pie were **against the law** in Kansas at one time.

There are 27 towns named **Walnut Grove** in Kansas.

A **hail stone** weighing 1.5 pounds (0.68 kilograms) once fell on Coffeyville.

Medicine bundles were sacred to Native Americans. They were used in important ceremonies and rituals.

Russell Stover was born in Kansas. He gave us the Eskimo Pie and Russell Stover candies.

The COWBOY Society **(Cock-eyed Old West Band of Yahoos)** of the Old West was formed to preserve the cowboy stories of Kansas.

The sea of prairie land is called "The Grassland Sea." It is home to more than **10 million insects** per acre (0.4 hectare).

Garden City is home to the **world's biggest hairball.** It was found in a cow's stomach at the packing plant.

Festivals

Celebrate!!!

International Pancake Derby, Liberal

Kansas Special Olympics, Wichita

Wichita River Festival

Beef Empire Days, Garden City

Mexican Fiesta, Topeka

Dodge City Days

Kansas State Fair, Hutchinson

St Lucia Festival, Lindsborg

Kickapoo Indian Powwow, Topeka

Flint Hills Rodeo, Strong City

Messiah Festival, Lindsborg

Eisenhower Center Open House, Abilene

National Flat-Picking Guitar Championships and Bluegrass Festival, Winfield

North Central Kansas Fair, Belleville

Czech Festival and Arts and Craft Show, Wilson

Holidays

Calendar

Martin Luther King, Jr. Day, *3rd Monday in January*

Groundhog Day, *February 2*

Presidents' Day, *3rd Monday in February*

Memorial Day, *last Monday in May*

Independence Day, *July 4*

Labor Day, *1st Monday in September*

Columbus Day, *2nd Monday in October*

Veterans Day, *November 11*

Thanksgiving, *4th Thursday in November*

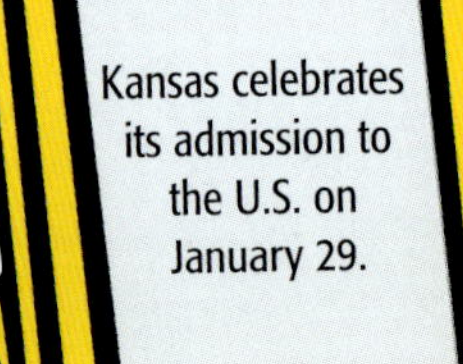

Kansas celebrates its admission to the U.S. on January 29.

Christmas, Chanukah, Kwanzaa, Vietnamese Tet, and Chinese New Year are all special celebrations in Kansas.

Famous Food

Kansas is famous for...

the following foods!

Pancakes	**Cherry dumplings**
Corn	**Fried pastries**
Ostrich steak	**Czech *kolaches***
Bran muffins	**Danish apple cake**
Round Steak	**Grated cheese potatoes**
Noodles with prunes	***Bierocks***
Cabbage Rolls	**Cottage cheese pockets**

Business & Trade

Kansas Works!

Kansas has a diverse economy with several major industries including Sprint, Boeing, Cessna, General Motors, and others. The many industries found in Kansas are very diversified. Kansans have a strong work ethic. They believe in working hard and in acquiring the skills necessary to succeed.

An important part of Kansas' economy is agribusiness. More than 21 million people work in agriculture providing food and fiber for people in the U.S. and in foreign countries. The aviation industry employs 22 percent of all manufacturing workers. Speciality items are also available in the state. Quilts, Swedish Dala horses, cowboy boots, and other unique items are made there. Mineral production provides jobs for people. Kansas is one of the top ten oil-producing states. Stone, salt, and helium are also important products.

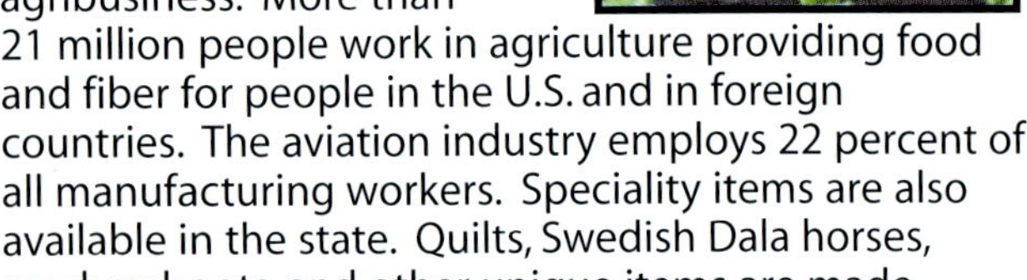

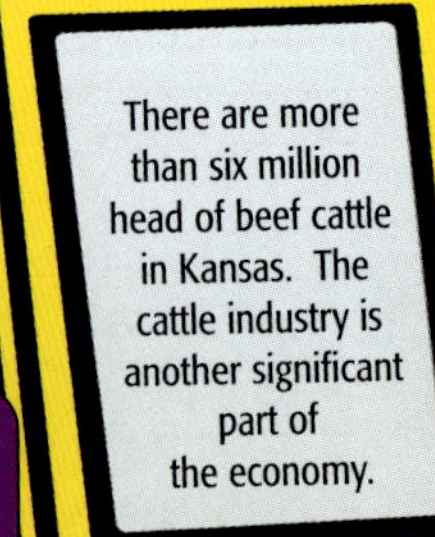

Kansas Books & Websites

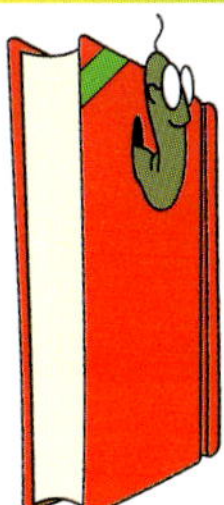

My First Book About Kansas by Carole Marsh
America the Beautiful: Kansas by Nancy Robinson Masters
Kids Learn America by Patricia Gordon and Reed C. Snow
Off the Beaten Path, Kansas by Patti Delano
Let's Discover the States: Kansas by the Aylesworths
The Kansas Experience Series by Carole Marsh

COOL KANSAS WEBSITES

http://www.state.kansas.us
http://www.kansasexperience.com
http://www.50states.com
http://www.netstate.com

Kansas Glossary

Glossary Words

agriculture: the science and art of farming

aviation: the science, skill, or work of flying airplanes

compromise: a settlement of a disagreement with both sides giving up something

contiguous: touching along all or most of one side

drought: a long period of dry weather with little or no rain

fanatical: overly enthusiastic

fowl: any bird

geographic center: center point of the 48 contiguous states

geodetic center: the continent's center point which includes adjustment measurements for the curvature of the earth

migratory: moving from one place to another

prairie: a large area of level or rolling grassland without many trees

sodbusters: people who moved to Kansas and built homes out of sod, mud, and grass

suffrage: the right to vote in political elections

temperance: the practice of not drinking any alcoholic beverages

Kansas

Here are some special Kansas-related words to learn! To take the Spelling Bee, have someone call out the words and you spell them aloud or write them on a piece of paper.

Spelling Words

- abolitionist
- Abilene
- agriculture
- bison
- buffalo
- constitution
- drought
- geodetic
- geographical
- homestead
- Kickapoo
- Leavenworth
- libraries
- natural resources
- Potawatomie
- reservoirs
- rodeos
- sodbuster
- Topeka
- Wichita

ABOUT THE AUTHOR...

CAROLE MARSH has been writing about Kansas for more than 20 years. She is the author of the popular *Kansas State Stuff Series* for young readers and creator along with her son, Michael Marsh, of *Kansas Facts and Factivities,* a CD-ROM widely used in Kansas schools. The author of more than 100 Kansas books and other supplementary educational materials on the state, Marsh is currently working on a new collection of Kansas materials for young people. Marsh correlates her Kansas materials to the Kansas learning standards. Many of her books and other materials have been inspired by or requested by Kansas teachers and librarians.

EDITORIAL ASSISTANT:

Jackie Clayton

GRAPHIC DESIGNERS:

Lisa Stanley Kathy Zimmer Al Fortunatti